NFL TODAY

THE STORY OF THE
DETROIT LIONS

THE STORY OF THE DETROIT LIONS

NATE LEBOUTILLIER

CREATIVE EDUCATION

Cover: Running back Doak Walker (top), wide
receiver Calvin Johnson (bottom)
Page 2: 1969 Detroit Lions
Pages 4–5: 1951 Detroit Lions
Pages 6–7: Wide receiver Calvin Johnson

....

Published by Creative Education
P.O. Box 227, Mankato, Minnesota 56002
Creative Education is an imprint of
The Creative Company
www.thecreativecompany.us

Design and production by Blue Design
Design Associate: Sarah Yakawonis
Printed in the United States of America

Photographs by AP Images (Carlos Osorio), Corbis
(Bettmann), Getty Images (Vernon Biever/NFL,
Scott Boehm, Clifton Boutelle/NFL Photos, Kevin C.
Cox, Tom Dahlin, Diamond Images, George Gelatly/
NFL, Walter Iooss Jr./Sports Illustrated, Dave
Kaup, Jeff Kowalsky/AFP, LC Larry Lambrecht/NFL,
Tannen Maury/AFP, Chris McGrath, Martin Mills,
Doug Monaco/AFP, NFL, NFL Photos, Betsy Peabody
Rowe/NFL, Pro Football Hall Of Fame/NFL, Robert
Riger, Joe Robbins, Andy Sacks, Michael Smith, Paul
Spinelli, Greg Trott)

Library of Congress Cataloging-in-Publication Data

LeBoutillier, Nate.
The story of the Detroit Lions / by Nate LeBoutillier.
p. cm. — (NFL today)
Includes index.
ISBN 978-1-58341-755-3
1. Detroit Lions (Football team)—History—Juvenile
literature. I. Title. II. Series.

GV956.D4L43 2008
796.332'640977434—dc22   2008022686

First Edition
9 8 7 6 5 4 3 2 1

CONTENTS

ON THE SIDELINES

MEET THE LIONS

HEAR THEM ROAR

Detroit, Michigan, was founded in 1701 by Frenchman Antoine de la Mothe Cadillac and became a major hub of transportation in the Great Lakes region. Located on Lake Erie, and with the Detroit River flowing through it, the city's early transportation relied on local waterways. But with the invention of the automobile, cars soon replaced boats as the preferred mode of transportation, and Detroit became the car capital of the world. It was here that automobile pioneer Henry Ford introduced the concept of assembly-line manufacturing in the 1890s. Today, this northern city is home to the three American car company giants—Ford, General Motors, and Chrysler—and is a major manufacturer of car parts and other steel products.

In 1934, the Detroit Tigers baseball team won the American League pennant and drew nearly a million fans—the best attendance record in the major leagues. "The Motor City" has also been known as a football town since 1934. That year, in the midst of the Great Depression, a radio tycoon and football enthusiast named George Richards bought a struggling National Football League (NFL) team called the Spartans and moved it from Portsmouth, Ohio, to Detroit. Renamed the Lions (a natural counterpart to the city's Tigers baseball club), the team has been on the prowl ever since.

X Detroit's auto manufacturing helped make it one of America's premier cities more than a century ago, and pro franchises such as the Lions made it a sports hotbed as well by the mid-1900s.

When the Lions settled in Detroit, the Tigers were the city's main sports attraction. But the Lions quickly got the attention of Michigan fans. The team had a powerful offense that featured such stars as running back Glenn Presnell and guard Grover "Ox" Emerson. In their first season, the Lions went 10–3, not allowing a single point in their first seven games. They also made national headlines by playing in a special Thanksgiving Day game—a Lions tradition that continues to this day.

In 1935, Detroit charged all the way to the NFL Championship Game. As freezing rain turned the University of Detroit Stadium field into a muddy mess, the Lions mauled the New York Giants 26–7 to become league champions. One of the stars of that game was quarterback Earl "Dutch" Clark, the first great Lions rusher and a player renowned for his cool leadership. "If Dutch stepped on the field with [football legends] Red Grange, Jim Thorpe, and George Gipp," an opposing coach once said, "Dutch would be the general."

The Lions remained a winning team for the rest of the 1930s and continued to add talented players in the years that followed. Detroit had some of the NFL's brightest stars in the 1940s, including Alex Wojciechowicz, an undersized but fierce center and linebacker, and Bill Dudley, a versatile

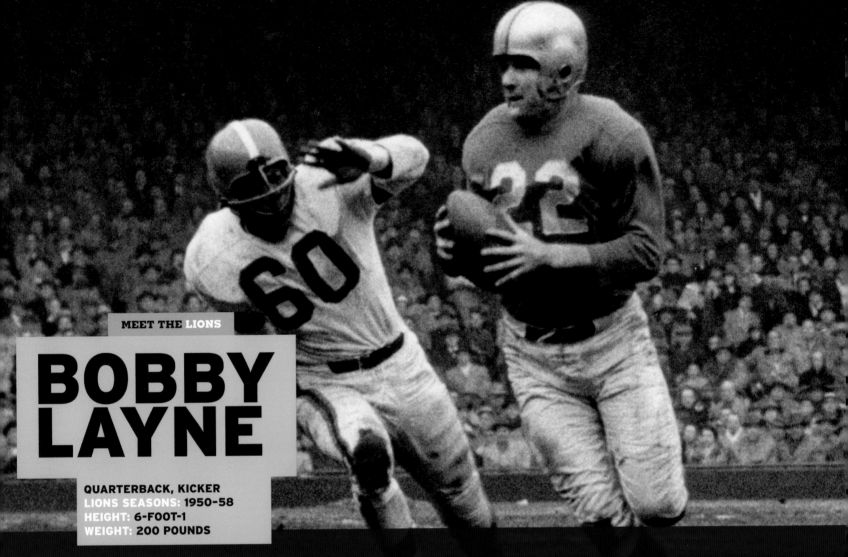

BOBBY LAYNE

QUARTERBACK, KICKER
LIONS SEASONS: 1950-58
HEIGHT: 6-FOOT-1
WEIGHT: 200 POUNDS

When Bobby Layne joined the Detroit Lions in 1950 by way of a trade with the New York Bulldogs, the Texan with the shock of blond hair had a reputation for late-night partying and underachievement. But Lions fans came to love the free-spirited quarterback, who would prove himself brilliant in the clutch and lead his team to three NFL championships. "Bobby Layne and television made Sundays bearable in this factory town," Detroit sports columnist Jerry Green said. "He was the symbol of this city, the toughest and best. He played without a face mask, and he was at his finest against the clock. When a touchdown drive was necessary, he could make the last two minutes seem an eternity." Layne's final full season with the Lions, 1957, was bittersweet. He led the team to the NFL Championship Game but couldn't play in it because he had broken a leg in the preceding game. The Lions traded Layne to the Pittsburgh Steelers two games into the 1958 season, and Detroit would win just 1 playoff game in the next 50 years.

Yet despite some great individual efforts, the '40s were

a difficult decade for Detroit. In 1942, the Lions went an

embarrassing 0–11. Twice during the decade, Lions teams

finished games in scoreless ties (in 1940 with the Chicago

Cardinals, and in 1943 with the New York Giants). In 1946,

1947, and 1948, Detroit finished in last place in the NFL's

Western Division.

Things finally began looking up in the Motor City in

1950. That year, the team acquired quarterback Bobby Layne

and signed a young running back named Doak Walker. With

the help of Leon Hart—a huge, remarkable athlete who

played both offensive and defensive end—the Lions went

a respectable 6–6. In 1951, after former Lions running back

Buddy Parker was named the team's head coach, Detroit

jumped to 7–4–1. Suddenly, the Lions were back.

The 1950s were a glorious era in Detroit, and the player

most responsible for those good times was Layne. Although

his career statistics in passing yards and touchdowns

were not overly impressive, Layne was a born leader

whose toughness was unmatched. He became fiery when

the situation called for it, but he preferred to inspire his

teammates with his calm attitude, often cracking jokes in the

As the Lions rose to power in the early 1950s, they developed one of football's first great rivalries versus the Cleveland Browns.

LIONS AND TURKEYS

In 1934, a businessman named George Richards purchased the Portsmouth, Ohio, Spartans professional football team, moved it to Detroit, and named it the Lions. The new Lions started the season 10–1. However, crowds at Lions games were paltry, especially when compared with the crowds at games of the Detroit Tigers, the city's popular pro baseball team. Richards tried thinking of ways to attract fans, and finally an idea came: Play a game on Thanksgiving Day. Richards and the Lions convinced NBC Radio to broadcast the game nationwide. It didn't hurt that the opponent that 1934 season was the undefeated Chicago Bears, the team's closest rival. A crowd 26,000 strong jammed into the University of Detroit Stadium, and several thousand others had to be turned away. The game (pictured) featured powerful Bears running back Bronko Nagurski on one side and the sparkling play of Lions quarterback Dutch Clark on the other. The Bears pulled out a 19–16 win, but a Lions tradition was born. With the exception of the World War II years of the early 1940s, Thanksgiving has been celebrated in Detroit every year since then with turkey and pigskin.

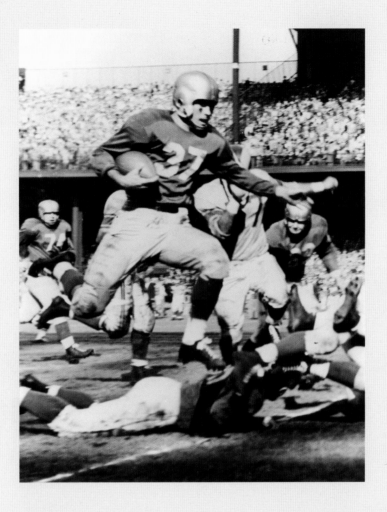

huddle during the tensest situations. Layne hated defeat and refused to believe his team could be beaten. "Bobby never lost a game," Walker once said. "The clock just ran out on him a couple of times, that's all."

In 1952, Layne, Walker, and Hart—along with star safety Jack Christiansen—led the Lions to a 9–3 record and the NFL Championship Game, where they faced the Cleveland

X Doak Walker played only six NFL seasons, but his amazing offensive versatility earned him a place in the Pro Football Hall of Fame.

Browns, one of the most consistently powerful teams of the '50s. In the title game, Walker broke free for a 67-yard touchdown run as Detroit won 17–7 to capture its first NFL championship in 17 years.

The Lions faced the Browns again in the 1953 NFL Championship Game, a contest that added to Layne's legend. With four minutes left in the fourth quarter, Cleveland led 16–10. In the Lions' offensive huddle, Layne saw nervousness in his teammates' eyes. "Now if you'll just block a little bit, fellas," he said in his confident Texas drawl, "ol' Bobby'll pass you right to the championship." Eight plays later, he threw a 33-yard touchdown pass, and the Lions were NFL champs for the second year in a row.

Layne led his team to the championship game again in 1954, but the Lions finally lost the title to the Browns. In 1957, the star quarterback suffered a broken leg. His backup, Tobin Rote, came in and led the way as Detroit won its fourth NFL title, crushing Cleveland 59–14 in the championship game. A year later, Detroit fans said goodbye to the greatest leader in Lions history when Layne was traded away.

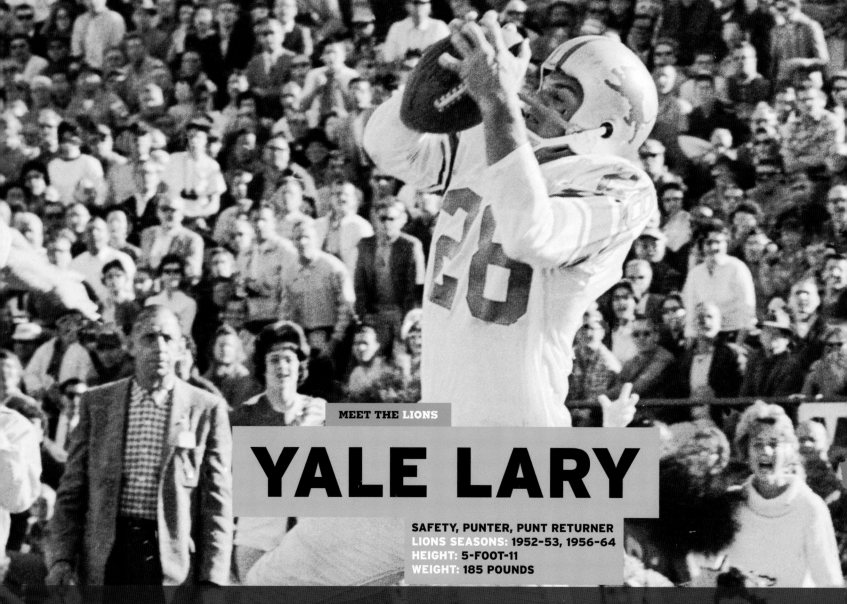

YALE LARY

SAFETY, PUNTER, PUNT RETURNER
LIONS SEASONS: 1952-53, 1956-64
HEIGHT: 5-FOOT-11
WEIGHT: 185 POUNDS

Yale Lary could do it all, and his career statistics prove it. Fifty career interceptions from his safety position show that he was an indispensable defender against opponents' passing attacks. A 44.3-yard punting average and an amazing streak of 32 consecutive punts without a return demonstrate that he was an exceptional punter. And three returns for touchdowns make clear that he was a legitimate weapon as a punt returner. But statistics don't tell the whole story of Lary's value. To actually witness Lary's lockdown pass coverage, his booming punts, and his electrifying returns was the best evidence. Lary's sense of overall duty to whatever job his team needed made him most valuable. His sense of duty to his country was equally strong, as he took time off from pro football to serve in the United States Army in 1954 and 1955. In all, the wiry Texan played 11 seasons in Detroit and was a key part of the Lions' NFL championship teams of 1952, 1953, and 1957. Nine of Lary's seasons garnered him Pro Bowl status, and he was inducted into the Pro Football Hall of Fame in 1979.

DEFENDING THEIR TURF

Without Layne, the Lions took a small step back, finishing second in the Western Conference in 1960, 1961, and 1962. The Lions had a fierce defense during those years. Linebacker Joe Schmidt's aggressive style made him a master of the "Red Dog" blitz play. Safety Yale Lary was one of the game's top ballhawks, making 50 interceptions during his Lions career. And cornerback Dick "Night Train" Lane earned a fearsome reputation as a headhunter for his habit of hitting opposing ballcarriers high and hard.

X Few defenders chased the ball with as much constant determination as Alex Karras; in 1960, 1961, and 1965, he was named an All-Pro as the best left defensive tackle in the NFL.

Another player who frightened opponents during these years was defensive tackle Alex Karras. At 260 pounds, Karras was as strong as an ox and capable of single-handedly collapsing offensive lines. But he was also incredibly fast and relentless in his pursuit. Offensive linemen could not match his speed; sometimes running backs couldn't, either. "Running away from Karras is worse than running at him," said Baltimore Colts running back Lenny Moore. "He moves so fast on those stumpy legs, and you can hear him closing in on you from behind. I hate that sound. You get this feeling like you're about to be buried by a buffalo stampede."

The Detroit defense proved just how good it was in 1962 during a classic Thanksgiving Day game against the 10–0 Green Bay Packers. The Lions swarmed all over the

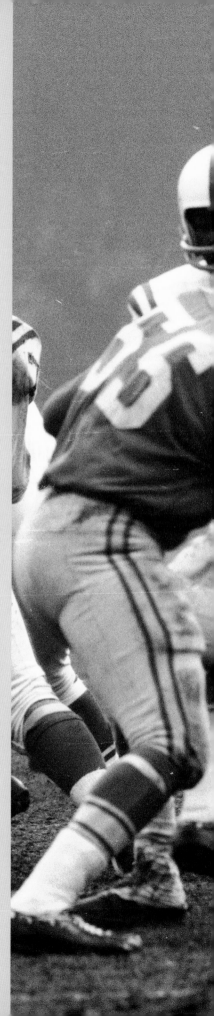

X Detroit's defense played with a fury in the 1960s, allowing fewer touchdowns than any other team in 1962 and 1965.

Packers' star quarterback, Bart Starr, sacking him 11 times throughout the afternoon. Detroit led 23–0 at halftime and won 26–14 in what one sportswriter in attendance called "one of the most memorable displays of aggressive defensive football ever witnessed."

But as good as the Lions' defense was, it was not good enough to bring Detroit another NFL title. After the team finished 1962 with an 11–3 record, victories were hard to come by the rest of the 1960s. Receiver Terry Barr and quarterback Milt Plum hooked up frequently to give the offense a lift, but

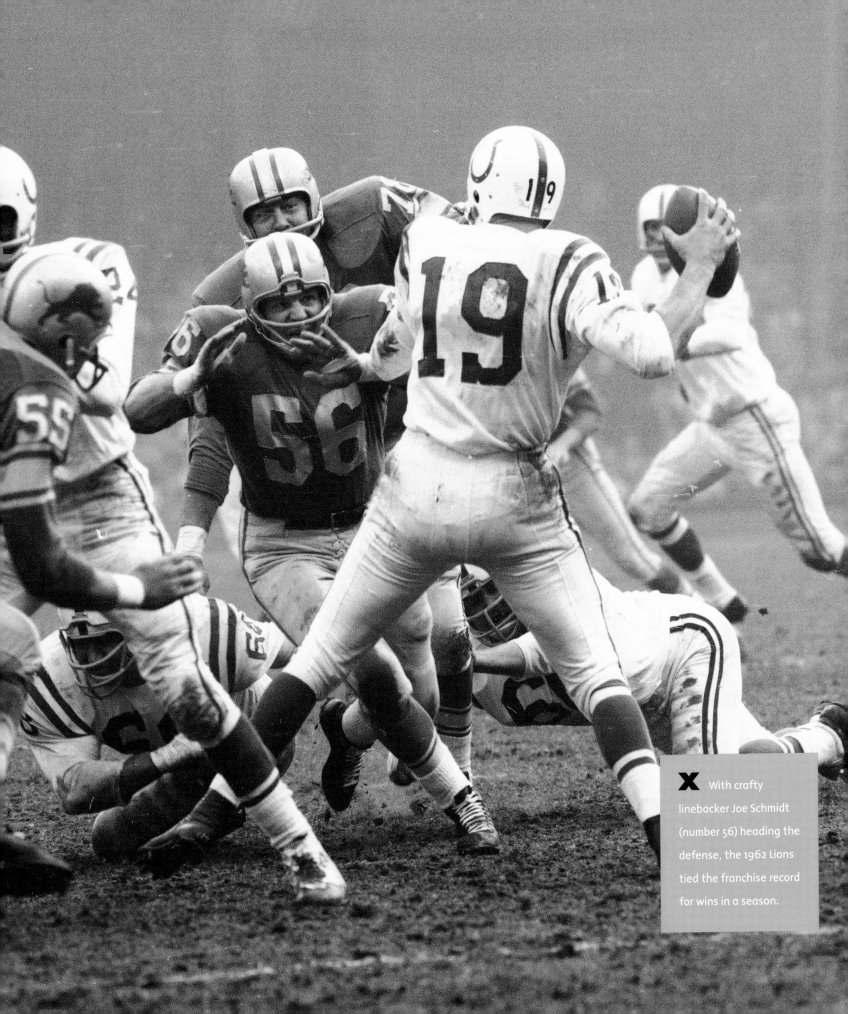

X With crafty linebacker Joe Schmidt (number 56) heading the defense, the 1962 Lions tied the franchise record for wins in a season.

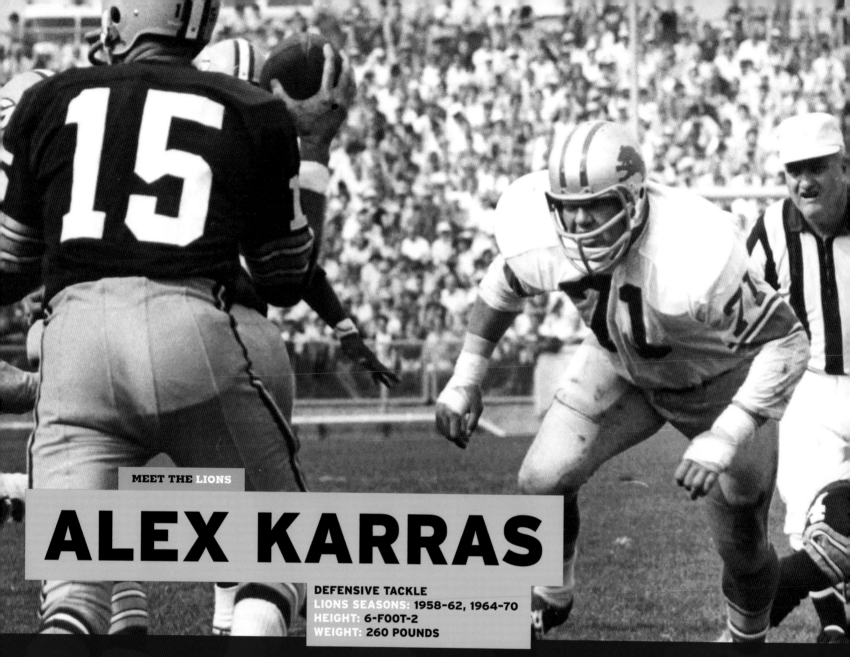

ALEX KARRAS

DEFENSIVE TACKLE
LIONS SEASONS: 1958-62, 1964-70
HEIGHT: 6-FOOT-2
WEIGHT: 260 POUNDS

Known for his career after pro football as much as his stellar play on the gridiron, Alex Karras was a true talent. Karras had a successful but disruptive college career at the University of Iowa. He played on both the offensive and defensive line for the Hawkeyes, but he had a rocky relationship with his coach, which caused him to periodically quit the team—then rejoin later. After Karras's college years, he briefly performed as a professional wrestler and then went on to star for the Lions, playing strictly defense. The Lions steadily improved, going 11–3 by 1962, but in 1963, Karras was suspended by the NFL for his involvement in a gambling ring at a bar he owned. After sitting out that season, Karras rejoined the Lions and spent seven more seasons chasing down running backs and wreaking havoc on opposing lines. Toward the end of his NFL career and after retirement, Karras went on to act in movies such as *Blazing Saddles* and *Paper Lion*, as well as the television sitcom *Webster*.

the team could never win the Western Conference to earn another shot at a championship.

As the 1970s began, the Lions were eager to return to championship form. They featured a number of new standouts during that time, including center Ed Flanagan, cornerback Lem Barney, and tight end Charlie Sanders. Unfortunately, the '70s proved to be frustrating years. The Minnesota Vikings ruled the new National Football Conference (NFC) Central Division throughout the decade, and Detroit finished second to the Vikings nearly every season.

In 1979, the Lions stumbled to a 2–14 record. The good news was that the poor record gave Detroit the first pick in the 1980 NFL Draft. With it, the team selected speedy running back Billy Sims, who had won the Heisman Trophy in 1978 as the nation's best college football player. The Lions hoped that Sims would provide the offensive boost they so badly needed.

Sims started his NFL career in fine style. In his first game, he scored 3 touchdowns, including a 41-yard run to pay dirt. During the 1980 season, Sims set a team record with 1,303 rushing yards, scored 13 touchdowns, and was named NFL Rookie of the Year. Behind Sims's performance, Detroit went 9–7. "I must admit," said Lions head coach

Monte Clark, "as much as I like to stress team effort, Billy has been the big difference."

Detroit continued to improve, making the postseason in 1982 and 1983. In the 1983 playoffs against the San Francisco 49ers, Sims scored two fourth-quarter touchdowns to put the Lions up 23–17 with five minutes remaining. But 49ers quarterback Joe Montana led his team to a late touchdown, putting the 49ers ahead 24–23. Lions kicker Eddie Murray tried a 43-yard field goal attempt with five seconds left to win the game, but he missed by inches, and the Lions lost. That would be the team's last playoff game for eight years.

The 1984 season was a disaster. The Lions lost several close games and went just 4–11–1, but worst of all, they lost Sims to a severe knee injury. He came back the next season but was never the same. As Sims's performance went downhill, the Lions went down with him. Running back James Jones and defensive end Michael Cofer did their best to keep the team competitive, but it wasn't enough. The Lions became one of the worst teams in football in the late '80s.

PAPER LION, ROARING WRITER

What's it like to stare across the line of scrimmage in the NFL from the quarterback position? Would an ordinary man shake in his cleats, scared that, should he drop back to pass, the snarling, grunting, 6-foot-6 defensive end would devour him and pound him into the turf? That, should he attempt to carry the ball on a bootleg, the 330-pound nose tackle or muscle-bound linebacker would crush his ribs with a single, bone-breaking hit? Author George Plimpton tried to convey the true NFL experience to the common fan in his book *Paper Lion*, an account of his participation in training camp with the 1963 Detroit Lions as a 36-year-old rookie quarterback. Plimpton was paid by *Sports Illustrated* to write about the overwhelming task of trying to become the Lions' third-string quarterback. In an intrasquad game, before he was cut, Plimpton got his chance to shine. He took the quarterback position for five offensive plays. On each one, the team lost yardage, but it didn't matter. Plimpton's book created a buzz, and in 1968, a movie was made based on the book.

SUPER SANDERS
TO THE RESCUE

NFL TODAY: THE STORY OF THE DETROIT LIONS

The 1989 season felt like 1980 all over again. With the third pick in that year's NFL Draft, the Lions found a new star. Like Billy Sims, he was a fast running back who wore number 20 on his jersey. His name was Barry Sanders, and he quickly proved that he was even better than Sims had been. On his very first carry, he shot through the line for an 18-yard gain. Sanders finished his rookie season by breaking Sims's team record with 1,470 rushing yards, although the Lions finished a mere 7–9.

Sanders was just getting started on one of the most amazing careers in NFL history. In his first six seasons, Sanders would rush for 8,672 yards—an average of 1,445 yards per year. And he did it in electrifying style. Sanders stood only 5-foot-8, but a combination of great balance, vision, and strength enabled him to spin, juke, and cut like no other runner in the game. "Barry is so good that sometimes during a game, I catch myself watching as a fan and not an opponent," said Tampa Bay Buccaneers

With an amazing, low-to-the-ground running style that made him a highlight waiting to happen, Barry Sanders captured the NFL rushing title four times (1990, 1994, 1996, and 1997). **X**

PLAYOFF POINTS AT A PREMIUM

It was 1970, and the Detroit Lions were back in the playoffs for the first time in 13 years. The Lions had a strong offensive attack, led by running backs Mel Farr and Altie Taylor (pictured), and they cruised into the playoffs by winning their last five games to finish the regular season 10–4. Their playoff adversary was Dallas, a team that had a reputation at that time for winning in the regular season but choking games away in the playoffs. Dallas's Cotton Bowl hosted the matchup, and defense was the name of the game. In the fourth quarter, the Lions had yet to score, and the Cowboys had only a field goal and a safety to show for their efforts. With less than a minute to play, the Lions drove to the Cowboys' 29-yard line, hoping for a game-winning touchdown. But it was not to be. The Cowboys intercepted a pass by Lions quarterback Greg Landry and won 5–0 in the lowest-scoring playoff game in NFL history. It would be another 12 years before Detroit would make the playoffs again.

linebacker Hardy Nickerson. "He does things that leave even pros' mouths hanging open."

Also starring in Detroit during the early '90s were tough linebacker Chris Spielman, swift kick returner Mel Gray, offensive tackle Lomas Brown, and receiver Herman Moore. Moore became one of the Lions' brightest stars after joining the team in 1991. The 6-foot-4 receiver had been an outstanding high jumper on his college track team, and he became known in the NFL for his ability to outleap defenders for high passes. These players led Detroit to a 12–4 record in 1991 and its first playoff game win since 1957, with a 38–6 victory over the Dallas Cowboys. However, the Washington Redskins dashed any Super Bowl hopes by trouncing Detroit 41–10 in the NFC Championship Game.

Detroit had a string of terrific regular seasons from 1993 to 1995. The playoffs, however, were a different story. In 1993, the Lions rode high with a 10–6 record and an NFC Central Division championship. In the regular season's final game, a home matchup against the Packers, the Lions roared to a 30–20 victory in front of a rocking Silverdome crowd. As fate would have it, the two teams were pitted against each other again in the Silverdome a mere six days later, this time for keeps. With Sanders running wild, the

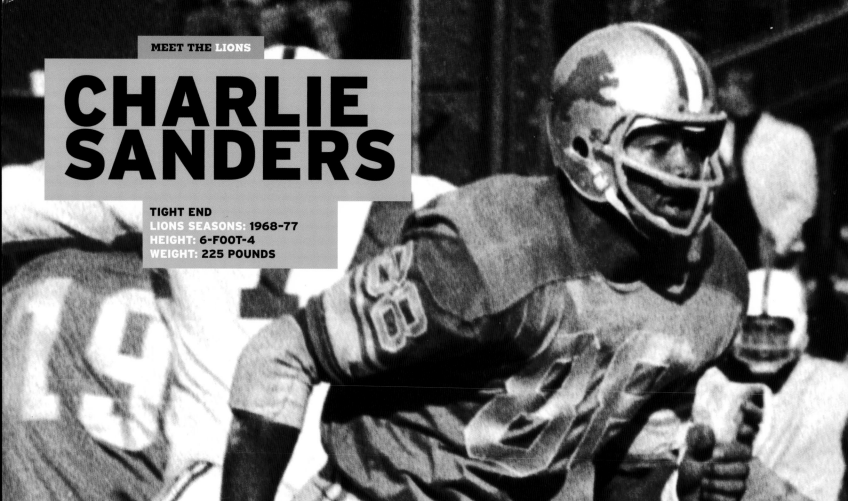

CHARLIE SANDERS

TIGHT END
LIONS SEASONS: 1968-77
HEIGHT: 6-FOOT-4
WEIGHT: 225 POUNDS

Charlie Sanders used to tape his thumb to his index finger during his sophomore season playing football at the University of Minnesota, and he became a defensive player because he couldn't catch the ball. But when team trainers discovered the reason Sanders was taping his hand—torn ligaments—they gave him the necessary medical attention, and Sanders went on to star as a receiver (as well as a basketball player) for the Golden Gophers. When the Detroit Lions chose Sanders in the 1968 NFL Draft, he gave the team an immediate boost, hauling in 40 receptions and throwing devastating blocks from his tight end position. The Lions' number 88 went on to play 10 seasons in Detroit, becoming the franchise's all-time leader in pass receptions (336) by the time he retired. "Charlie was totally selfless when giving up his body, and he would make these phenomenal catches," said team owner William Clay Ford at Sanders's 2007 Hall of Fame induction ceremony. "He caught your eye. Charlie is what you look for today in a tight end. He was a pioneer at the position."

Lions led 24–21 late in the fourth quarter. But the Packers,

behind quarterback Brett Favre and receiver Sterling

Sharpe, mounted a comeback that culminated in a Favre-

to-Sharpe, game-winning touchdown pass that gave

Green Bay a 28–24 victory and shocked the big crowd into

disappointed silence.

A year later, the Packers knocked the Lions from the

playoffs again, this time 16–12, with Green Bay holding

Sanders to negative-1 yard on 13 carries. With 1:51 left to

play, Moore caught a desperation pass to the end zone

X Herman Moore
was arguably the NFL's
best receiver in the
mid-1990s, catching
more than 100 passes
in 1995, 1996, and 1997.

but stepped just out of bounds, and he lamented the loss afterward. "This is one of those games that is going to kill you to sit back in the off-season and think about," he said. "It's disappointing. I just hope we can bounce back from it, because we have a good team here."

The Lions did bounce back in 1995, going 10–6 as Sanders rushed for 1,500 yards, Moore caught an NFL-record 123 passes for 14 touchdowns, and quarterback Scott Mitchell threw a team-record 32 touchdown passes. But the Lions were stung in the first round of the playoffs yet again with a 58–37 loss to the Philadelphia Eagles in the highest-scoring playoff game in NFL history.

The late '90s were years of great individual achievement in Detroit. On the heels of Moore and Mitchell's records in 1995, Sanders charged for 2,053 rushing yards in 1997, becoming only the third running back ever to top the prestigious 2,000-yard mark. But despite these outstanding efforts, Lions fans were left feeling shortchanged when it came to postseason fortunes.

RIDING THE WIND

In November 2002, the Lions played their biggest rivals, the Bears, in Chicago. With the score tied 17–17 after four quarters, the game went into overtime. NFL rules state that a coin toss determines which team gets to decide who will kick off, who will receive, and which ends of the field the teams will defend. The first team to score wins. The Lions won the coin toss. But instead of electing to receive, as teams virtually always do, Detroit head coach Marty Mornhinweg elected to "take the wind" and let the Bears receive the ball first, hoping the stiff breeze would force the Bears to punt and leave Detroit with good field position. The Bears promptly marched down the field for the winning score. Mornhinweg remained unapologetic afterwards. "The people who were there and know all the information know that it was the right call," he said. "It was the right call then, it's the right call now, and it's the right call 10 years from now." Lions fans thought otherwise, and at season's end, Mornhinweg was fired.

TOUGH TIMES
IN D-TOWN

X- -

The Lions were dealt a stunning blow in 1999 when Sanders announced his retirement. Although he was only 30 years old and needed just 1,458 yards to surpass former Chicago Bears great Walter Payton as the NFL's all-time rushing leader, he felt the timing was right. "I always told myself I would play this game as long as it was fun," he explained. "When it became a job for me, I decided it was time to move on."

Since injuries had also slowed Moore, the Lions were forced to find some new stars. Over the next few seasons, Detroit fans cheered for such players as receiver Germane Crowell, linebacker Stephen Boyd, running back James Stewart, and quarterback Joey Harrington. In 2002, these players and the rest of the Lions left the Pontiac Silverdome—the team's home since 1975—and moved into Ford Field, a beautiful new stadium in downtown Detroit.

The Lions struggled in the first few seasons of the 21st century, going 2–14 in 2001 and 3–13 in 2002. Two key additions came aboard in 2003 hoping to boost Detroit up the standings in the new NFC North Division. First, the team hired a new coach: Steve Mariucci, who had previously built a winning record as coach of the 49ers. Then the Lions selected Charles Rogers, a tall and fast receiver

CHRIS SPIELMAN

LINEBACKER
LIONS SEASONS: 1988-95
HEIGHT: 6 FEET
WEIGHT: 250 POUNDS

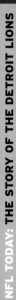

One of the true football warriors of his day, Lions linebacker Chris Spielman treated fans to a hard-nosed brand of football. Detroit selected Spielman in the second round of the 1988 NFL Draft, and he started all 16 games that year as the anchor of the defense, leading the team with 153 tackles. Spielman gained a reputation for doing whatever it took to gain an advantage, from pushing himself through extra workouts to watching hours of tape. "If he thought sleeping in his uniform would make him better, he would do it," said Don Cleamons, a Lions linebackers coach. Spielman was selected to the first of four career Pro Bowl teams in his second season. As Detroit found success in the early 1990s, Spielman's penchant for bone-jarring hits rivaled his offensive counterpart Barry Sanders's knack for crowd-pleasing runs. In addition, Spielman just *looked* tough; it seemed he always had some fierce-looking facial hair and splatters of blood on his jersey or pants. Whether the blood was his own or someone else's, opposing quarterbacks and ballcarriers knew one thing: they wanted to stay clear of number 54.

from nearby Michigan State University, in the NFL Draft. In college, Rogers broke many school records, including career touchdowns (27), and he entered the league as a "can't miss" prospect. Unfortunately, Rogers was beleaguered by broken collarbone injuries in his first two seasons with Detroit and could never regain his fine collegiate form as a pro. Harrington also muddled through some erratic years at the quarterback position.

Beset by poor play, injuries, and bad luck, the Lions remained in a hole. In an unusual team-building strategy, they selected receivers with high first-round draft picks three years in a row and limped to records of 5–11 in 2003, 6–10 in 2004, and 5–11 in 2005. Five losses in 2005 were by five points or fewer, but even close losses were still losses.

X Michigan native Steve Mariucci's hiring as head coach in 2003 gave Lions fans hope, but he could not lift Detroit out of its slump.

X A 350-pound monster of a defensive tackle, Shaun Rogers was capable of single-handedly dominating the line of scrimmage.

Many fans began calling for the head of Matt Millen, the team's general manager and president. During the 2005 season, the Lions fired Coach Mariucci instead.

Mariucci's replacement was Rod Marinelli, who had been a defensive assistant coach for the Tampa Bay Buccaneers. Savvy veteran Jon Kitna was signed to play quarterback, and Kevin Jones became the team's featured running back. Young receiver Roy Williams put forth some exciting performances, but the team's defense was weak, and the 2007 season couldn't come fast enough for Lions fans as Detroit struggled to a 3–13 mark in 2006.

The "Silver and Blue" added still another receiver with the second overall pick of the 2007 NFL Draft: Calvin Johnson from Georgia Tech. Johnson was big, speedy, and sure-handed, and early training sessions between him and Kitna got the quarterback so excited that he made a prediction on a local radio station. "I'll keep to myself what I think we actually will win," he said. "But it's more than 10 games."

The Lions made Kitna look smart by starting out 6–2 in 2007. The veteran led the charge, willing the team to victories with timely throws and a leadership that hadn't been recognizable in a Lions quarterback in decades. The defense seemed rejuvenated, spearheaded by tackle and team

X Although his team was frequently outmatched, Jon Kitna (right) did what he could, completing an NFL-high 372 passes in 2006.

captain Cory Redding and aggressive linebacker Ernie Sims. But then the team collapsed, losing six straight games and limping to a 7–9 finish. Injuries to many key offensive players didn't help matters, but that didn't lessen the disappointment.

The selection of offensive tackle Gosder Cherilus in the first round of the 2008 NFL Draft signified a change in philosophy in Detroit. "Is he a glamour guy?" Coach Marinelli

DOME IS WHERE THE HEART IS

On October 6, 1975, the Lions ushered in a new era in Detroit: indoor football. The Lions had shared Tiger Stadium with the city's major league baseball team since 1938. The Silverdome, with its 80,311 seats, became the NFL's largest stadium. The Lions lost their first game in the Silverdome by a score of 36–10 to the Cowboys, and although the team never experienced overwhelming success there, millions of fans enjoyed the controlled climate. In the next 10 years, more domes popped up across the NFL, including the Louisiana Superdome in New Orleans, the Kingdome in Seattle, the Metrodome in Minneapolis, and the RCA Dome in Indianapolis. The Silverdome also hosted other entertainment, such as Detroit Pistons basketball games, immense rock concerts, the 1979 National Basketball Association All-Star Game, and Super Bowl XVI in 1982. In 1987, a record crowd of 93,173 assembled in the Silverdome to watch Wrestlemania III. That same year, Pope John Paul II even conducted a Catholic Mass there. In 2002, the Lions left the Silverdome for a new domed stadium, Ford Field (pictured).

A PLAYOFF GAME TO REMEMBER

Between 1957 and 2008, the Detroit Lions won just a single playoff game. But what a sweet victory it was. The 1991 Detroit Lions finished the regular season with a 12–4 record, good for first place in the NFC Central Division. They had a young star at running back in Barry Sanders, an upstart quarterback in Erik Kramer, a talented receiving duo in Herman Moore and Brett Perriman, and a stout defense that was anchored by All-Pro linebacker Chris Spielman. When the Dallas Cowboys came to town, 78,385 fans packed Detroit's Silverdome to show their support. The Lions pounced early with a pair of touchdowns and a field goal for a 17–6 halftime lead. Kramer threw for 2 more scores, and Sanders sprinted 47 yards for a late touchdown to punctuate the Lions' 38–6 win. The Silverdome was a boisterous bubble of cheers as the game's final seconds ticked away. Unfortunately for Detroit, the road to the Super Bowl was blocked by the Washington Redskins in the NFC Championship Game a week later as the Lions got walloped, 41–10.

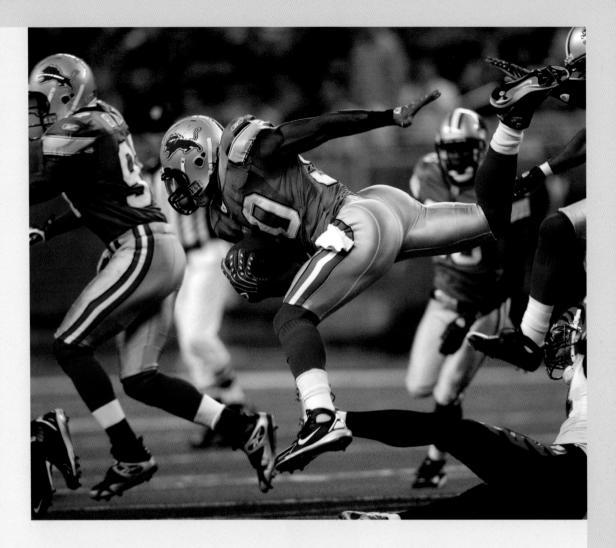

asked of Cherilus. "No. But for a coach he is." The Lions

would need much more than the gritty Cherilus in 2008,

though. When Detroit started 0–3, Millen was finally fired.

But that didn't stop the bleeding. In what turned out to be

the worst team season in NFL history, the 2008 Lions went

an unprecedented 0–16, getting blown out in many games.

Marinelli was fired, and Detroit was left at rock bottom, with

nowhere to go but up.

X Swift linebacker
Ernie Sims was one
of the cornerstones
of Detroit's effort to
reestablish itself as a
defensive powerhouse.

X The Lions' 2008 season turned out to be a test of character, as Detroit became the first NFL team ever to lose all 16 of its games.

BARRY SANDERS

RUNNING BACK
LIONS SEASONS: 1989-98
HEIGHT: 5-FOOT-8
WEIGHT: 203 POUNDS

Barry Sanders was almost certainly the most electrifying running back ever to lace up cleats in the NFL. The jitterbugging halfback burst onto the NFL scene after a stellar collegiate career at Oklahoma State University, where he won the 1988 Heisman Trophy, awarded to the best college player in America. The Lions drafted him in 1989, and Sanders went on to rush for more than 1,000 yards in each of his 10 pro seasons (gaining 15,269 yards total). Sanders's ability to change directions while sprinting at full speed was simply captivating, and his moves left shocked defenders clutching empty air between their fingers instead of his number 20 jersey. When he reached the end zone, there were never spikes or dances; the quiet star simply handed the ball to the referee. The Lions never possessed an overwhelming defense or much of a passing attack during Sanders's tenure, which helps explain why the Lions won just a single playoff game during that period. Nevertheless, the chance to see Sanders in action made watching every Lions game worth it during those years.

With an all-time roster that includes such names as Layne, Lary, and Sanders, the Detroit Lions have featured their share of NFL greats. Yet in the five decades since winning their fourth NFL championship in 1957, the Lions have won only one playoff game. Today's Lions, settled in Ford Field and hungry for respect, hope to soon pounce on a Super Bowl trophy and make The Motor City a town of champions once again.

The Lions hoped for big things in the future from Cory Redding, who became one of the NFL's highest-paid defensive tackles in 2008.